JOURNEYS

Reader's Notebook
Volume 1

Grade 2

Houghton Mifflin Harcourt™

Copyright © by Houghton Mifflin Harcourt Publishing Company

All rights reserved. No part of this work may be reproduced or transmitted in any form or by any means, electronic or mechanical, including photocopying or recording, or by any information storage and retrieval system, without the prior written permission of the copyright owner unless such copying is expressly permitted by federal copyright law. Requests for permission to make copies of any part of the work should be addressed to Houghton Mifflin Harcourt Publishing Company, Attn: Intellectual Property Licensing, 9400 Southpark Center Loop, Orlando, Florida 32819-8647.

Printed in the U.S.A.

ISBN 978-0-544-59261-2

24 0928 23 22 21

4500821214 CDEFG

If you have received these materials as examination copies free of charge, Houghton Mifflin Harcourt Publishing Company retains title to the materials and they may not be resold. Resale of examination copies is strictly prohibited.

Possession of this publication in print format does not entitle users to convert this publication, or any portion of it, into electronic format.

Contents

Unit 1

Lesson 1:	Henry and Mudge	1
Lesson 2:	My Family	16
Lesson 3:	Dogs	31
Lesson 4:	Diary of a Spider	46
Lesson 5:	Teacher's Pets	61

Unit 2

Lesson 6:	Animals Building Homes	76
Lesson 7:	The Ugly Vegetables	91
Lesson 8:	Super Storms	106
Lesson 9:	How Chipmunk Got His Stripes	121
Lesson 10:	Jellies: The Life of Jellyfish	136

Reader's Guide: *Poppleton in Winter* 151

Unit 3

Lesson 11:	Click, Clack, Moo: Cows That Type	155
Lesson 12:	Ah, Music!	170
Lesson 13:	Schools Around the World	185
Lesson 14:	Helen Keller	200
Lesson 15:	Officer Buckle and Gloria	215

Reading and Writing Glossary G1